Hoofbeats

&

Heartbeats

Printed by Imprint Printing Services 2005

printing@imprint-deeside.co.uk

Published by Riding for the Disabled

Typeset in 12 point Garamond

ISBN 0-9542076-4-5

© Authors

All rights reserved. No part of this publication may be reproduced, stored in a retrieval system, or transmitted, in any form or by any means, electronic, mechanical, photocopying, recording or otherwise, without the prior permission of the Copyright owners.

RDA

The Riding for the Disabled Association incorporating Carriage Driving

Registered under Charity Number 244108

President: HRH The Princess Royal KG GCVO

The RDA is a Federation of Independent Groups administered through a National Office through Regional and County Committees. Nationally, the RDA currently has 534 groups and 23,000 disabled riders and carriage drivers. As a voluntary organisation it is people-power intensive: riders and drivers' participation is dependent on the support of some 14,000 committed and dedicated helpers. Being 'horsey' is not a prerequisite of being a volunteer help is also required with administration, fundraising and sometimes transport. There are three regions in Scotland. Grampian & Highland Region covers a huge geographical area and the nineteen groups within the region provide riding and driving for hundreds of individuals. Each RDA group operates as a registered charity in its own right, from Forfar in the south of the region, to Orkney in the north, Skye & Lochalsh in the west and Buchan in the east. Some branches are very small, with only a handful of riders or drivers, and others have very large numbers of regular participants. The oldest group in the area was established as far back as 1970, and the most recent addition was set up in 2003.

RDA offers an activity that is suitable for virtually all ages with special needs, and qualified Group Instructors and AB Whips are trained to cope with all types and levels of disability. Adults and children are encouraged to take part in the RDA experience and through it benefit from increased independence, confidence and self-esteem. Improved communication and social skills are also reported by parents, teachers and carers, as well as better balance, co-ordination, concentration and co-operation. The riders and drivers enjoy their regular exercise in relaxed atmosphere of fun and companionship, and the benefits of supervised activity in a safe, outdoor environment are second to none.

The proceeds from the sale of this book will enable groups to continue providing quality riding and carriage-driving opportunities for people with special needs.

Inspiration for this fundraising compilation of poems came from Shirley Cruickshank's original work, which she kindly gifted to Buchan RDA Group. Some of her poems are happy, some funny and some sad – but they are all thought provoking. Everyone who has ever been near a horse and anyone who has ever felt close to any animal, will appreciate this book.

"RDA - Improving Lives…"

Headquarters –
Lavinia Norfolk House
Avenue 'R'
Stoneleigh Park
Warwickshire
CV8 2LY

Telephone   024 7669 6510
e-mail   rdahq@riding-for-the-disabled.org.uk
website   www.riding-for-the-disabled.org.uk

Contents

No Fear	09
Special Needs	10
Fun for All	11
Horse Riding	12
Illustration by Emily Bell	13
Tuesday Morning	14
Positive Thinking	16
Honey	17
Buzby	18
Illustration by Ally Milne	19
The Longest Hours	20
Sam	21
Happy Treks	22
The Good Old Days	24
Illustration by Craig Grant	26
Pet Trails	27
Katie Kitten	28
Riding the Highland Way	29
If I Could Turn Back Time	30
Horse Whispers	32
The Cottar House	34
Who's to Blame	35
Hamish	36
Animals	37
Illustration by Daryl Stephen	38
The Tale of Harry Owl	39
Hartpury	40
For Johnny	42
Illustration by Michael Burnett	43
Photograph of Alfie	44
Alfie	45
The Mysterious Voice	46
Alfie	47
Alfie the Horse	48
Alfie	49
Alfie	50
Alfie the Horse	51
Alfie is a Very Lovely Horse	52
Alfie Came to School One Day	53
Illustration by Connor Jane	54
The Dog Fun Day	55

My Wish	56
Empty Days	57
Not Now	58
Illustration by Rhys Leslie	59
Bye for Now	60
A Horse Called Memories	61
We Were There on That Day	62
War Horses	63
Meals on Wheels	64
We Owe it to Them	65
Gnome Sweet Gnome	66
Trinkets of Tears	67
Horse Hunting	68
Illustration by Aonghas Pettitt	70
Commitment	71
Things to Come (I Hope!)	72
The Glory of Competition	73
Testing Time	74
Illustration by Grant Cooper	76
The Grand Fund Raising Auction	77
Wish You Were Here	78
The Horse Owner's Year	79
But!	80
My Black Eye	81
Phantom Gypsy	82
The Aftermath	83
Clip Clop	84
Illustration by Michael Smith	85
Copper's Christmas Lights	86
Last Christmas	87
Working in a Winter Wonder Yard	88
Last Christmas	89
Illustration by Jamie Penny	90
Christmas Wish	91
Oh Winter Time	92
Winter's Tale	94
Bob the Cob	95
Two Pounds and an Apple	96
Illustration by Stacey Cheyne	97
Join the Group	98
Illustration by Richard Gray	99
About Shirley Cruickshank	100

This book was compiled by
Mrs Susan Fowlie & Mrs Barbara Gibbons
Regional Publicity Officers for the
RDA Grampian & Highland Region

We would like to pay thanks to the following:

Mrs Shirley Cruickshank
for the gift of her poems

The Craigmyle Community Ltd
for their generous grant

1V Horse
(www.4horse.co.uk)
for their support

RDA Volunteers
without whose contribution RDA could not operate

NO FEAR

His wheelchair bumps across the stones,
His head is turned around.
He's frightened, and he's only small
And then he hears the sound…

A noise he hasn't heard before,
A loud - clip - clop - clip - clop.
He looks up at his carer
As if to say, 'Please stop'.

A soft-eyed horse is standing there,
It lowers down its head.
He thinks it's going to hurt him,
But it blows warm air instead.

His frail thin hand then reaches out,
It meets a velvet nose.
His frightened look just melts away,
Instead his smile now grows.

He's lifted up, it feels so high,
He knows that he won't fall.
When there's loving arms to hold him,
And the horse that knows it all.

Shirley Cruickshank

SPECIAL NEEDS

Oh God of creatures living
I offer you a prayer
For all your special children
You entrust now to our care
Some with twisted bodies
Some locked inside their mind
But all such untold freedom
Can with a pony find

Eyes glistening now with pleasure
They come aboard to ride
The wheelchairs sit abandoned
And sticks are thrown aside
Would anybody blame us
If we should smugly say
It takes a very special Pony
To be used for R.D.A.

Shirley Cruickshank

FUN FOR ALL

Smiley faces, eager arms,
eyes bright with happy tears –
released now from the prisons
that have held them all those years.

A life of being the odd ones out,
the ones who miss the fun;
the ones dependent all the time –
since they can't play or run.

A whole new world just opened up,
as free now as the rest.
They banter in their innocence
about which horse is best.

They sit aboard, their heads held high,
with helpers either side.
No longer told they can't do that
they're doing it – they can ride!

It brings a purpose to their lives
this group called R.D.A.
So let's hear it for the helpers then!
Yes – HIP HIP HIP – HOORAY!!!

Shirley Cruickshank

HORSE RIDING

Strapping on my hat
Waiting for my turn
I want to ride Copper
through the woods
I can hear Copper grunting
waiting for me.

I Love my horse.

Connor Jane
RDA Driver

Me and Paddy'

Emily Bell RDA Rider

TUESDAY MORNING

Have I got a good deal for you;
a morning, a week, out of school.
When the weather is fine,
far away from the grind,
said the Boss, taking me for a fool.

Off we go in the school mini-bus,
on approach to Raemoir I suss.
They'll be piebald, skewbald and roan,
I'm fighting the urge to run home.
Oh no, this is scary, I fuss.

Who'd want to ride on a horse?
Eager children and nutters, of course!
To ride Piper, Hobo, and Sable?
If I'm honest I'm only just able
to reign rising terror by force.

The helpers are full of caffeine,
the lads with their hats on are keen,
to gallop or canter or trot.
I'm weak at the knees at the thought,
just the prospect's turning me green!

The boys each mount a steed,
around the arena by lead,
sometimes on a hack,
before long they're back,
little enticement they need.

In a flash, it seems to me, it's Noon.
Me frightened? Nah don't be a goon!
On reflection it's not really so bad,
in fact I'm very nearly glad,
it'll be Tuesday morning again soon!!!

Tracey Ritchie
(nervous Linn Moor helper)

POSITIVE THINKING

When you think you are beaten – you are.
When you're too scared to try – you don't.
When you'd love to win but you think you can't –
It's a sure thing that you won't.
When you think you're the worst – you are.
Think positive and rise.
You've got to feel that you're good enough
Or you'll never win a prize.
When you're scared to lose – you've lost.
For in all events we find –
Success begins with how we feel
It's all a state of mind.
Life's trophies seldom go
To the richest or fastest man.
So often you'll find that the one who wins
Is the one who thinks he can!

Shirley Cruickshank

HONEY

Fridays are exciting days
I'm going horse riding
Honey my friend
Silky coat hooves clip-clopping

Honey never makes me sad
I hear the wind whistling
And Carol shouting instructions
I feel warm skin and her soft mane.

Craig Grant (Age 9)
RDA Rider

BUZBY

Buzby loves Polos and hay
And apples and carrots
And I love him.

I love winning games
On his strong back.

I love his shiny conker coat
And walking in the woods
Hearing his hooves clatter.

He is my kind friend and I'm
thinking –
I'm good at this.

Ally Milne (Age 9)
RDA Rider

Ally Milne (Age 9)
RDA Rider

THE LONGEST HOURS

It's cold and dark, the hours drag past.
I'm tired, I need to sleep.
Just how long can one night last?
Still, this vigil I must keep.
So many things that all need doing–
I'll plan them now to stay awake.
Order feed, and book the shoeing–
Still I stay here for her sake.
Then– I sense she needs me,
At once I'm by her side.
Gently coaxing, speaking quietly,
My heart is bursting now with pride.
Forgotten is my weariness,
My tears now freely flow.
Just how much I love her,
No-one will ever know.
I hear her softly whicker,
Come on, get on your feet.
As she nuzzles at her new born foal,
So perfect and so sweet.
At last I make it to my bed,
As daybreak fills the sky.
And realise that someone else
Now needs her more than I.
Tomorrow she will show him off
For all the world to see.
Tonight there's room for no-one else,
Just him– not even me.

Shirley Cruickshank

SAM

Feeling happy having fun
Everything is all right
When I'm riding Sam my horse
His coat as black as night

I hold out a Polo in my hand
He takes it with velvety lips
I'd love to ride Sam on the sand
And splash through all the waves.

Stacey Cheyne (Age 9)
RDA Rider

HAPPY TREKS

Away up in the Highlands where tourists like to go,
Is a little riding centre, like many more you know.
The ponies there are very cute, they trek out nose to tail,
The only paces that they know are 'very slow' and 'snail'.

One pony in particular is loved and known by all,
He's black and white and hairy and he isn't very tall.
A little girl she lost her heart to Mac on holiday,
Her parents said they'd buy him, good money they would pay.

They duly came to see him, to see what he could do.
Yes, he could trot and canter, and jump a small fence too.
Young Suzy said she'd ride him, and with little legs wrapped tight,
He never once did misbehave (but looked as though he might!)

When they rolled up in their horse-box, no-one shed too many tears,
Which puzzled the new owners— he'd been a favourite there for years.
I thought it fair to tell them that he's known for his strong will,
But was warned off by the owner— if only looks could kill!

A loving pat from all the kids and they told him with a smile—
Mac— enjoy your holiday, we'll see you in a while.
All went well for the first few days till Mac wanted some fun—
Then when they tried to catch him, round in circles would he run.

They'd shut him in his stable but by morning he'd be out,
Mac is in the feed shed, became the usual shout.
He'd prance around and stand on toes as they put on his tack
But wouldn't move, he stood stock still, when they got on his back.

Despite their best intentions, Mac was not a happy lad,
So they felt they must return him— they couldn't bear him sad.
We told them, **Please, don't be upset, you gave it your best try** —
When Mac came prancing down the ramp a glint was in his eye…

Now he's home— plodding round, doing things he seemed to miss,
He loves when kiddies hug his neck or give him a big kiss.
Though we think he must be bored, doing the same thing each day,
For Mac, it's just his way of life and that's the way it'll stay.

Shirley Cruickshank

GOOD OLD DAYS

When first of all I owned a horse— back in prehistoric days,
Things were done so differently, in oh so many ways.
Indoor schools were quite unknown, and outdoor schools were rare.
Essentials were a velvet hat and a yellow shirt to wear.
Schooling was done out in the field. Jumping— over broken gate.
Long days I'd spend there with my horse, from morning until late.
No herbs were added to their feeds, no supplements or chaff,
Just pony cubes and broad flaked bran and oats (now that's a laugh).
I never had a back man, nor a saddle fitter call.
The vet came when I needed him and the blacksmith— that was all.
No riding club to help me then, and though the pony club was there,
My parents had no time to go, and I really didn't care.
The roads seemed safer then to ride, the cars all slowed right down.
My horse was good in traffic so I rode him through the town.
No one near had horses, so I'd hack out all alone.
How did I ever manage without a mobile phone?
I enjoyed my horse. I loved him loads— he was no angel though.
Let him see an open space and off flat out he'd go!
He never wore a rug till he was old; he lived outside all year.
He hated being stabled and he made it very clear.
We went through so much together, from grass-sickness he fought back.
In those days cobs weren't fashionable and his hairy feet took flak!
I'll never forget Paddy. His memories are real.
Sometimes if Jene nuzzles me, it's Paddy's nose I feel.

Twenty-three years later came the day we said goodbye.
At the age of thirty-seven, he went to pastures in the sky.
Horse owning was so different then, peer pressure there was none.
Back then the most important thing was— RIDING SHOULD BE FUN!

Shirley Cruickshank

Craig Grant (Age 9)
RDA Rider

PET TRAILS

Does your Granny have a cat
that curls and sleeps in her best hat?
Maybe yours will have a dog
that snores whilst sleeping like a log.
A budgie, did I hear you say,
that chirps and whistles all the day?
Well on my Granny's fireside rug
is her pet, a great big slug!
The vegetables he eats aren't much,
he doesn't need a cage nor hutch.
He crawls around with silver trail,
he's much more handsome than a snail.
He's very long and very fat,
he'd terrify the bravest cat.
With his horns stretched out to the full,
he's rather like a tiny bull.
Yes, Sammy Slug is granny's pet,
the quietest one you'll ever get.
At night he sleeps beneath the sink,
it is much nicer than you'd think.
In the morning out he comes
to nibble all the toasty crumbs.
But don't call to visit him today,
She's taken him on holiday!

Shirley Cruickshank

KATIE KITTEN

Katie was a kitten cat
That sat upon the kitchen mat.
Though in her dish were all things nice,
Her favourite food was furry mice.
Sunny days would find her there
Asleep in the grass without a care.
But if rain was pouring to the ground
The kitten cat could not be found.
Out in the farm on bales of straw
I climbed and looked, guess what I saw?
She yawned and blinked and looked at me,
Oh what a cosy place to be!

Shirley Cruickshank

RIDING THE HIGHLAND WAY

Please don't look at me like that, I know you're only small.
Compared to all those stags and things, I weigh nothing at all.
Right, now I'm up, you're very short. Stand still a minute, please.
Something it seems is missing, oops, your head's between
  your knees!
Must we jog? You're like a kid that's just got out to play.
Still, you're popular for trekking, and are safe rides so they say.
Renowned for placid natures, with eyes like liquid pools,
Highlands may be gentle, but for sure they ain't no fools!
I try my legs to bend you round, but mine are bent round you.
Bouncy trot steps, up and down— just slow down, please, will you?
At last it's time to head back home, a cutie there's no doubt—
You look at me as if to say, what's all the fuss about?
I think we'll have some real fun times, but you've pulled my
  fingers numb.
However much my legs might ache— they're better than my bum!!!

Shirley Cruickshank

IF I COULD TURN BACK TIME

If I was granted now three wishes I wouldn't have a clue
Of what I'd have and what I'd not, I don't know what I'd do.
But if someone said go back in time for just a little while,
I'd know exactly where to go and run off with a smile.

It's five o'clock, the morning's dark, the frost lies a' aroon.
Can ye hear the tacketts on my beets, they fairly mak a soon.
Through the doors an in the stalls the bonniest pair ye've seen.
They're a' that maks ma life complete, Black Jock and Bonny Jean.

They whinny fin they ken it's me, a richt gweed noise they mak.
I brak the ice, syne gie them corn and pit hay in their rack.
I brush them ower and tie their tails, then let them hae a doze.
Tae the bothy I'll gan back the noo and sup ma bowl o' brose.

I'll pit the collars ower their heids and turn them roon tae fit.
I tak the harness fae the wa', the bridle and the bit.
Jock's fair champin' at his bit, I think we're ready noo.
We'll donner aff up tae the park and there I yoke the ploo.

Trampin' up and doon for a' the day, ahint my lovely pair,
Jet Black Jock, the muckle lad, and Jean ma bonny mare.
An' then I'll feed and bed them doon and see that they're a richt.
I'll gie their big thick manes a clap and leave them for the nicht.

Excuse me now—I think I hear the tractor in the yard.
Bang on cue, as if to prove a farmer's life is hard.
He needs the phone, he wants to call the tractor service man.
Says, "Afternoon would be okay—but sooner if you can.

Of course I think it's serious, that's why I call you now.
The cab's computer's broken down and just won't set the plough!"
The tractor roars off down our road, as big as I have seen.
But it doesn't hold a candle— *to Black Jock and Bonny Jean!*

Shirley Cruickshank

HORSE WHISPERS

I'd swear that it's not often—
just every now and then,
there comes a horseman with the know-how
of ten ordinary men.

You'll never hear him boasting
of the value of his way,
but he's figured out those horses' minds
and learnt the games they play.

He's well at ease among them,
he can read what's in their head.
I'd swear that if a horse could talk
he'd know just what it said.

I've seen him work with troubled ones,
with ones not keen to please,
but with gentleness and patience
he can ride them round with ease.

I've witnessed many owners
ride their horses in his style,
and hope now that his laid-back ways
will stay with us a while.

It's not just how to ride a horse,
he'll teach you horsemanship,
you and your horse will think as one—
no need to use a whip.

His method is an attitude
that stems from deep inside.
His theories open up
a whole new kinder way to ride.

He has the knack of showing you
how to use the skills he knows.
His easy, friendly manner
is so special— and it shows.

'Join up', trust and patience,
and a little common sense.
Meet him if you can — and learn —
a **Whisperer** has the know-how of ten ordinary men.

Shirley Cruickshank

THE COTTAR HOUSE

How many tired and aching bones have rested in your bed?
How many crying babies in your cradle needing fed?
What conversations spoken round your fire on evenings dark?
Before they bedded themselves early, to be up before the lark.
How many heavy footsteps have entered through your door?
How many barefoot children have played upon your floor?
Whose calloused hands produced the rugs of brightly
    coloured rags?
The same hands that filled the girnel with the oatmeal from
    the bags?
How many hearty bowls of broth were cooked upon your range?
How many desperate tears were shed when they saw that things
    would change?
How many evening hours were spent sewing samplers for
    the walls?
How many tiny child hands helped roll oatmeal into balls?
I sit here, and I wonder, and I feel you all around,
And the ticking of your mantel clock is now the only sound.

Shirley Cruickshank

WHO'S TO BLAME?

There's an *intme* comes to our yard. Perhaps you have one too.
It does all the things that good horse owners wouldn't do.
It borrows without asking, and never puts things back.
I know if it were my place, I'd be giving it the sack.
It leaves the feed room door unlocked, and lets the pigs get in,
So when you go to make up feeds, they've emptied every bin.
It scatters rubbish everywhere around the tack room floor,
And never ever seems to read the notice on the door.
Please— clean up after your horse, is all it has to do.
But no, the floors are left— looking like a horsey loo!
It's left the field gates open, so the horses all got out.
It's never there to offer help, or hear you if you shout.
It's left forks lying in the passage, and barrows in a pen.
It will get round to moving them, but never says just when.
Oh yes— I know it comes here, though its face I never see—
Ask anybody, **Who did that?** And they'll say, **It wasn't me.**

Shirley Cruickshank

HAMISH

Hamish is a Haggis and he lives up in the hill,
And you can only see him if you sit so very still.
You will see the bracken moving and hear a rustling on the ground—
Then you'll know he's coming and you'll hear a chuckling sound.
Far behind the bushes a small shape soon appears,
He's small and round, he has a snout and tiny pointed ears.
He has a little bonnet and he wears a tartan kilt,
Just listen to him singing in his lovely highland lilt.
He always seems so happy, look at him run and twirl,
Now he does the sword dance— all the while his bagpipes skirl.
But night is nearly over and dawn is creeping in,
He knows he'll have to leave you soon and rubs his whiskered chin.
Hamish trudges up the hill, back up the narrow track,
When he's almost reached the top, he pauses to look back.
He knows that you can see him, even with your eyes closed tight,
He waves and shouts, **You'll see me in your dreams tomorrow night!**

Shirley Cruickshank

ANIMALS

Cats, horse, gerbils and dogs,
Tigers, lions, meerkats and warthogs,
These are only a few,
Dolphins, whales and kangaroos too.

Mouse, hamsters, hedgehogs and bats,
Rabbits, foxes, squirrels and rats,
There is never a bore,
There are a lot more.

Cows, weasels, badgers and hares,
Sheep, pigs and lambs make me stare,
Camels, giraffes and snakes,
Everyone is great mates.

My favourite is dolphins and dogs,
My dog plays with fire logs,
I've never seen a dolphin but they are so cute,
They make noise like a flute.

Kirsty Robertson,
Contributor

Daryl Stephen (Age 9)
RDA Rider

THE TALE OF HARRY OWL

Harry was the only owl who didn't give a hoot,
He sat up in the rafters, decked in his three piece suit.
He didn't catch a single mouse, it would cramp his style would that,
He just whispered down instructions to the poor worn out farm cat.
One day the farm cat he complained to the farmer who was Boss.
He said, **Old Harry's got to go, I can't afford the loss.**
He gets his wage and never moves his bottom off that beam—
I'd be cheaper with another cat and another bowl of cream!
The farmer said, **Look Harry, I've warned you twice before.**
So now old boy, I'm sorry, but I'm showing you the door.
Harry swivelled round his head, then went to pack his bag,
He strolled slowly through the door, and got in his brand new Jag.
As he screeched off down the motorway, a tear was in his eye—
Then he thought that he felt peckish and would like a mousemeat pie.
When he pulled in to the Diner and sauntered on inside,
A pretty chick from up the way, she begged him for a ride.
She climbed into his speed machine, this chick was so impressed.
She said she liked his looks, his style, oh, and the way he dressed.
She said she was a battery-chick, but looking for a change,
Harry said that he was unemployed— in other words Free Range!
His money soon was all run out, his chick she flew the coop.
No well-done steaks for Harry now, just a little bowl of soup.
The car was sold, his suit in rags, a really tatty lad,
But beneath his matted feather coat, he wasn't all that bad.
He bought the papers every day and searched for jobs in vain;
Would Harry ever get to be a gentleman again?
Someone to answer telephones, thought Harry, that will do,
The only words he had to say were, **You'd like to speak to whooo?**
He worked so hard and earned so much, they all called him Sir Harry—
And then last week he bought himself a brand new red Ferrari!

Shirley Cruickshank

HARTPURY

To Hartpury we did go
Our driving skills to show
The competition was very tough
Nonetheless we did our stuff

The Dressage Judges were severe
Many a driver shed a tear
Prince and Donal both did well
It's just our Ben Hurs we should sell

The Cones were set with great precision
We needed now to make the decision
Which cones were narrow and needed more care
And which we could drive with a bit more flair

Then at last the Marathon day
A wonderful course before us lay
The hazards they were big and tight
The water really a great delight

Unfortunately we did not win
Perhaps we needed a double gin
But charming people we did meet
At Hartpury College in the heat

Ruth I know deserves a mention
For coping with my bouts of tension
And thanks to Rosemary Di and Pat
For pushing me up hills and flat

Last not least a great big ***Thank You***
To all Group members old and new
For making this my dream come true
Next time perhaps it may be YOU.

Kathleen Penny
RDA Driver

FOR JOHNNY

This is a very special day
For a donkey both loved and admired.
He's been living and working with Jean all his life
Now they both think it's time they retired.

Johnny started Carriage Driving for Disabled,
In Dunkeld, with all of his friends.
It's now nation-wide and such a success
That even the 'Royals' attend.

At shows, events and championships,
He stands out from the rest.
At Lowther and Stoneleigh, <u>the</u> elite,
He beat the very best.

So, a Happy Birthday Johnny,
From all of us here today.
And for you and Jean, such devoted friends,
Health and Happiness all the way.

Jean Emslie
RDA Driver

Michael Burnett (Age 5)
RDA Rider

Alfie

ALFIE

Alfie so big and strong

So that he can carry me.

His eyes so soft and gentle look at me and say,

Hello I will look after you.

His ears so pointed and big

Turn listening for his name.

His red and blue coat

Kept him warm.

His brown and white hair

Was so soft when I stroked him.

I know I am safe on his back

When I look at his big feet.

Class 9

THE MYSTERIOUS VOICE

Clippitty, cloppitty,
Clippitty, cloppitty,
Listen to that noise.

Clippitty, cloppitty,
Clippitty, cloppitty,
Could it be our boys?

No— Stuart is busy counting,

Kieran's colouring in,

Bryan and Robbie are looking at books...

Oh — Anthony — why that grin?

Look.
We have a visitor -
Alfie's come round past.

Alfie's shoes made that clip-clop noise,
The mystery's solved— at last!

Class 3
RDA Riders

ALFIE

Alfie came to our school

On a rainy day.

He trotted round the playground

Looking for some hay.

We patted and we petted him

And gave him food to eat.

He went home quite delighted

With his Anna Ritchie treat.

Class 11
RDA Riders

ALFIE THE HORSE

Alfie is big and white like a cloud
Little patches of brown
Feet clip-clopping
In the playground
Everywhere he goes

A sound sound sounds.

***Stewart, Lucas and Aodhan (Class 4)
RDA Riders***

ALFIE

Alfie, Alfie,
Horse so big and strong,
We heard your hooves
As you trotted along.

Alfie, Alfie,
Perhaps you're not very old,
But you were well behaved
And did as you were told.

Alfie, Alfie,
You liked to munch
On apples, carrots and mints
And your teeth went crunch.

Written by Class 5
RDA Rider

ALFIE

Alfie,

We always

Look forward to horse-riding.

You are

Friendly and faithful,

Important to

Everyone

At the Anna Ritchie School.

Class 7
RDA Riders

ALFIE THE HORSE

All white with brown patches
And feet hard and noisy
We could hear him moving
Along in the rain
His coat was soft and smooth
With his big yellow teeth.

Jamie and Sam
Class 4

ALFIE IS A VERY LOVELY HORSE

He came to school one day
Hours in the playground he did stand
Recruit from the R.D.A.
Standing proud and smiling
Everyone pleased he came

Children standing all around
And stroking his long white mane
Ladies led him round about
Laughter filled the air
Eating apples from their hands
Delight he was there

A brilliant day was had by all
Leaving him was sad
Furry funky fearless
In him a friend we had.

Class 6
RDA Riders

ALFIE CAME TO SCHOOL ONE DAY

Alfie came to school one day,

Munching on a bunch of hay.

The children wanted him to stay,

Mrs Cruickshank said, *No Way.*

The R.D.A. took HER away,

And left Alfie, HIP HIP HOORAY!

Class 8
RDA Riders

Connor Jane (Age 9)
RDA Rider

THE DOG FUN DAY

We gathered on Sunday at Overhall Farm
To show off the charms of our pets.
I will tell you below how they used all the 'Charm',
With never a thought or regrets.

In the 'Tail Wagging' class they all sat on their tails,
The owners were in such a fuss.
The dogs were just trying to make a small point,
'It's you that are stupid not us'.

In 'Appealing Eyes' class they all went to sleep,
Kept their eyes tightly shut of course.
If husbands and wives behaved like our dogs,
Half the country would sue for divorce.

The Agility Course was a great big success
For the humans, much more than the dogs.
They zigzagged and jumped and crawled round the course,
Like a troop of demented, large frogs.

Next year for a change we'll have 'Owners' Fun Day'
And the dogs can just sit back and grin.
The biggest event will be 'Veterans' class,
Whoever stands up longest will win.

Jean Emslie
RDA Driver

MY WISH

If the day should come when I'm in pain,
And you know I won't be well again,
Promise you'll do what must be done,
If this is the battle that can't be won.
It'll break your heart but please be kind,
Don't let your grieving sway your mind,
For this is when you'll let me see
Just how much you do love me.

Together we've had happy years,
The future now can hold no fears.
Please don't let me suffer – so
When that day comes, just let me go.
For my usual vet please will you send,
But stay with me until the end.
Hold me steady; speak to me,
Till my once bright eyes no longer see.

In time I hope you'll come to see
It's the last good deed you'll do for me.
One more time please stroke my mane,
And know that I'll have no more pain.
And don't be sad that it was you
Who decided this was what to do.
We've been such buddies through the years,
Don't let me be the cause of tears…

…You'll always see me graze now, the sun upon my back.
Painful limbs won't tire me now, however long the hack.
I live now in your heart and mind, a lovely place to stay,
And what you have in memories, no one can take away.

Shirley Cruickshank

EMPTY DAYS

Just going through the motions, surviving day by day.
Nothing holds much meaning, now he has gone away.
Confusion, anger, sorrow, are emotions that you feel.
The hands of time are ticking, and they tell you time will heal.

You wonder why this had to be, why fate was so unkind.
Was there anything you could have done? Nothing springs to mind.
Was it really only yesterday you had to let him go?
It seems a million years ago, and how you miss him so.

You can't look in the stable, it's cold and empty now.
The pails and rugs so neatly stacked look out of place somehow.
You expect to hear him whinny as you walk towards his door;
You long to see his handsome face, but you cannot any more.

You know you gave him all the love that you had there to give.
Ben knew that he could never have a better place to live.
That doesn't mend your broken heart or stem the tears that flow,
But someday it will help you I've been there, and I know.

Written for Iain Smith's " It's Benjamin " a.k.a. " Ben "

Shirley Cruickshank

NOT NOW

Please, oh please don't take him now,
Allow me one more day.
There's so much I want to do for him,
So much I need to say.
I need to brush his glossy coat
And comb his flowing mane.
Because once you take him from me, Lord,
I can't do it again.
I need to ride him out once more,
The wind blowing in our hair.
Why do you need to take him?
You know it isn't fair.
I have to hug him close to me,
And breathe his special smell.
If you take him it will break my heart,
Lord, surely you can tell.
Not all our prayers are answered,
You took him anyway,
You knew I'd never let him go,
If you'd let me have my way.

Shirley Cruickshank

Rhys Leslie (Age 9)
RDA Rider

BYE FOR NOW

There is a land that's mystical,
A place where time stands still,
A valley where the grass is green
And sunlight warms the hill.
A place where all God's creatures
Can rest when life is done,
And all of them are special,
Yes, each and every one.
Dogs and puppies can run and play
Without hunger or pain.
The oldest horses prance about
Like they were foals again.
Someday I'll glimpse that haven
When my days on earth are through.
And again I'll hug the furry friends
That in this life I knew.
So, till then my dear old horses,
My corgi, cats and chows,
My gerbils and my hamster,
I'll just say, ***Bye for now.***

Shirley Cruickshank

A HORSE CALLED MEMORIES

At first light I would see you, curled-up and lying there,
Velvet nose against the grass, you hadn't got a care.
Every time that we rode by, you'd prick your ears and neigh,
Our mares would call out-back to you, and we'd be on our way,
A silhouette in moonlight, bathed in pure white light,
That's always how you looked to me, if I passed by at night.
Not long ago I watched you, it seems like yesterday –
You raced around and played the clown, just like a foal at play.
Then fate stepped in, she played her card, she played it cruel and fast,
Grass sickness took a hold of you – just days then did you last.
So handsome, kind and able, a very special lad.
You're gone now – it seems so unfair – it really makes me sad.
Admired by all who saw you, sorely missed still that is true,
You truly were just lovely – a horse that once I knew.

Originally this poem was written for Maverick & Malley, Niel Gillander's horses that died in 2002. But I now dedicate it to the memories of all the horses that have been taken by this dreadful illness. My thoughts are with everyone who has been affected, and those of us fortunate not to have been.
We just have to treasure and enjoy every second with our horses because we never know what's just around the corner.

Shirley Cruickshank

WE WERE THERE ON THAT DAY

Endless hours of grooming, till our coats were shining bright,
Harness placed on silently and fitted up just right.
Hooves were oiled and polished, we had a special role to play,
For a very special lady, on this the saddest day.
Six of us were chosen, an honour, that we know.
But if all of us were honest, we just didn't want to go.
Us, without a muscle moving, some men with eyes brimmed full,
Gently placed upon the carriage, the precious cargo we would pull,
Out into the sunlight, flower scent heavy in the air.
But not as heavy as the hearts of all the people there.
They felt that they had lost a friend, a light gone from their lives,
As mothers hugged their children, and husbands held their wives.
Slowly, oh so slowly, with her coffin, flag and flowers,
As if a jolt might wake up this Princess Di of ours.
We'd never seen the crowds so huge, nor heard so many weep,
As they gazed in silence, on a sight for memory to keep.
We quietly pulled up at the gate, our task now all but done.
We had served our Princess well that day, as we stood there in the sun.
Then the bell tolled solemnly for all the folk to hear.
That's when along with all the world six – horses shed a tear.

Remembering Diana, Princess of Wales and her companion, Dodi Fayed, who died 31st. August 1997. Also Henri Paul who died at the accident scene.

Shirley Cruickshank

WAR HORSES

Think of winters twice as cold as any we will know.
Imagine that for endless months your world is only snow.
The sky is filled continually with screaming fighter jets.
Gunfire sounds; tanks rumble by. You're terrified – and yet,
Somewhere in the midst of this, in bullet riddled stalls,
Is a sight to weaken the most hardened hearts of all.
A stud of Lipizzaners have survived through all the hell,
And a little bit about them in this poem I now tell.
There are stallions, mares and youngsters, all pure, once full
   of grace,
Now only haunted, staring eyes look out from their white face.
Their faithful grooms have had no wage, they do this out of love,
And every night they pray for help from their good Lord above.
Those creatures once magnificent now live from day to day,
As they pick at bowls of dusty corn and scraps of mouldy hay.
They don't think they can cope much more, but bravely face
   their fears.
The stallions haven't been outside – not once – in five long years.
The I.L.P.H. heard of them and their action plan did start.
Everyone they mentioned it to, took it to their heart.
Soon the aid was flooding in; cash and goods and men.
They got out there to Bosnia, and acted there and then.
The situation at the stud is really looking good.
The vets and farriers have been and most of all – there's FOOD!
The horses are now feeling bright and get outside to graze,
The Bosnian Lipizzaners made it through to better days.
(Details of Bosnian Lipizzaners appeal can be had from
I.L.P.H.)

Shirley Cruickshank

MEALS ON WHEELS

Packed in together, nowhere to run,
Why am I here – what have I done?
So hot and so dark, how I long to see sky,
I feel so afraid, if I could I would cry.
I was loved once by children, it seems not long ago
That they'd drag me along to show after show,
Kicking me on when I needed to rest;
I never objected, I just gave of my best.
I'd come home the hero, rosettes all hung up,
So proud when they said, **Misty won us a cup.**
Then the children lost interest, I was left out to graze –
But still taken care of – oh wonderful days.
Then yesterday came, I was taken away,
I thought it would be somewhere nice for the day.
It seemed like a show but with something not right,
I didn't go home with my family that night…
About two days later they opened the door:
The little grey pony lay dead on the floor,
Along with a skewbald, a black and a bay –
But those ones were lucky, they died on the way.
The rest endured HELL to face only slaughter,
They were once loved by someone maybe – your son
   or daughter.

Shirley Cruickshank

WE OWE IT TO THEM

They stand in the paddock, their heads held low.
Huddled together, they watch darkness grow.
The mud that they wade through gets deeper each day,
So dirty, you can't tell the white from the bay.
If they are lucky, they are brought inside.
But not for some love – just for someone to ride.
Not for them fussing – no grooming, no treat,
Nobody cares about shoes for their feet.
There are some who love them, some people who care.
They act as their voice, the few people who dare.
Their owners don't like us – say, **Keep your nose out.**
They hurl their abuse, and they scream and they shout.
But WE must protect them, we MUST be their voice,
We make decisions, but they have no choice.
They put their faith in us, they give us their trust,
To ensure their wellbeing, I feel is a must.
If you see horses and all is not well,
Always remember, there's someone to tell.
Look in the phone book, there are numbers to call.
THE HORSES DESERVE IT, EACH ONE AND ALL.

Shirley Cruickshank

GNOME SWEET HOME

Stop and think this Wintertime of those who have no home,
Of down and outs, of refugees, and Fred the wandering gnome.
Fred once had a rockery where he lived without a care,
Till they sold the garden as a plot, and built a new house there.
He thought they soon would rearrange, find him another place,
But when he woke up by the bin, knew this was not the case.
A good gnome's not kept down for long, he gathered his small load,
Tied it in a handkerchief and Fred he hit the road.
He got very, very worried about when the snow would come,
More than just three inches and he had a cold wet bum.
Crossing roads was difficult, with legs that were so short,
It meant he had to sprint them, and he wasn't good at sport.
Tired and hungry Fred sat down, to rest his legs a while.
A blackbird sat beside him, Fred offered a tired smile.
Hop on my back, she said to Fred, *I'll take you to a friend,*
She lives in Olive Cottage in a street called Causewayend,
She cares for all the animals but I'm sure she'll care for you.
So on he got, and straight for Coupar Angus they now flew.
She gave him mince and tatties, the gnomies' favourite food.
Fred he looked at her and said, **OH MY, BUT THAT WAS GOOD!**
You're welcome Fred, said Sheila, when the gnome he tried to speak,
Just tidy my small garden up on Tuesdays every week.
Fred still works, but not so hard, because he's now quite old,
But it's still a lovely story and the first time it's been told!

Name of gnome has been changed to protect identity from
Gnome Office officials)

Shirley Cruickshank

TRINKETS OF TEARS

How could you kill an elephant
to make a statuette?
Leave a calf without a mum,
oh, wait there's still worse yet.
To take its tusks with axe and saw
when the beast is still alive.
Greed is the only reason,
to see a business thrive.
To see the anguish of the cow
when a friend she tries to save.
The nightmares that the calves will have,
will haunt them to their graves.
Shot down by poisoned arrow
or killed by poacher's gun –
they watch their family falling,
as they kill them one by one.
To decorate a glassy shelf
or make a pretty dish,
it's wrong to use the ivory tusks,
so I only have one wish.
To stop it now while there's still time,
the message is so plain.
Then at least the mighty elephants
will not have died in vain.

Shirley Cruickshank

HORSE HUNTING

Not so many years ago, when looking for a horse,
I said it had to be a bay and gelding – well of course.
My first horse she had been a mare, I didn't keep her long.
So gelding it would have to be – they could do no wrong!

I tried a big bay Warmblood that reared and bucked and spun.
I tried a chestnut thoroughbred, and the quarter horse was fun.
I went to see a dapple grey – so thin, with big, sad eyes.
The big black shire cross sounded nice – but never at that size!

We drove for miles, my patient spouse was getting pretty bored.
Anything I seemed to want, I just could not afford.
Looking through 'The Scottish Farmer' I saw an advert there,
Everything was perfect – except it was a mare!

However when I saw her I knew she was for me.
I thought she was so beautiful, the best there'd ever be.
My love for her had blocked it out, my heart had ruled my head.
I never bought a gelding – I now own a mare instead!

Every month she got so moody, a right stroppy little horse.
All her problems I put down to being a mare of course.
She'd jog past geldings, tail held high, flirting with each one,
While I just hung on terrified and she thought it was fun!

The scatty mare I used to have is gone I'm pleased to say.
With age has come maturity she's learnt along life's way.
Five years on I know her well, her bad days and her good,
What she'll do and what she won't, depending on her mood!

Now with youngsters we hack out and she shows them how it's done,
That cattle aren't scary and from cars no need to run.
Every horse is precious, each will have its special job.
But there's not a horse in this whole world that I'd trade for my COB!

Shirley Cruickshank

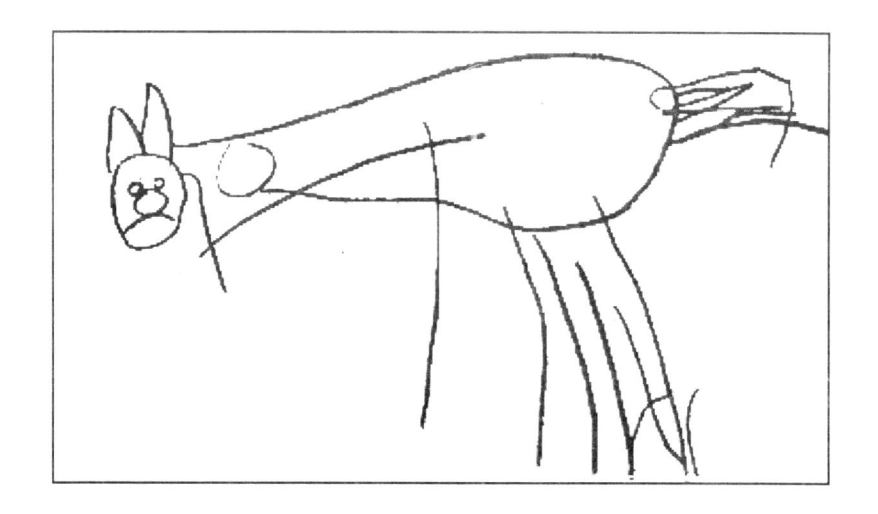

Aonghas Pettit (Age 7)
RDA Rider

COMMITMENT

Making the decision that you want to own a horse
Is like marriage – you will take him on for better or for worse.
It's not always an easy road to travel at the start –
Sometimes it goes so badly wrong it almost breaks your heart.
You'll buy him this, you'll feed him that, you'll treat him like a god,
But try to get up on his back, he's just a proper sod.
Sell him now, he'll kill you, is often the advice;
Still underneath you know there is a horse that could be nice.
There will be tears – you'll cry them in the silence of the night.
Your head will argue with your heart that maybe they are right.
Then comes the day you realise he hasn't bucked or napped,
He's trotted past the polythene although it blew and flapped..
Take it slow he'll trust you just a little more each day –
The bond is surely forming in its very special way.
Stick with it – you can do it – it's worth it in the end,
You chose him, and he's going to be your loyal, lifelong friend.

Shirley Cruickshank

THINGS TO COME – (I HOPE!)

We trot around amongst the jumps,
My heart just full of dread,
My knuckles white against the reins
And legs that feel like lead.
She bounds along, her head tucked in,
To her it's just a game,
When then the dreaded sound it comes,
And someone calls my name.
We see the poles loom up ahead,
I try to keep in line,
I'd really like to go home now –
But she doesn't give me time.
One, two, three – her stride is right,
We rise up now as one.
We land again – I'm still on board –
This jumping sure is fun!
The poles are up, they didn't fall,
That means we jumped it clear.
I hug her long black mane and say –
We did it – in a year!
Oh – did I say – it wasn't Wembley,
Where we soared up to the sky.
But our first lesson with the Riding Club
And the jump just one foot high!

Shirley Cruickshank

THE GLORY OF COMPETITION

It's five thirty in the morning, by six we'll be away,
Check all the equipment, brushes, rugs and hay.
Last night was just chaos, heaps of tack to clean,
Every piece was caked in mud, wherever it had been.
Jackets brushed and shirts all neat, hair nets for our hair,
Nice white jodhpurs, shiny boots, all ready now to wear.
First-aid kits all packed away, and boxes for our lunch,
Cups for us and pails for them, and carrots they will munch.
Five to six we must go now. Come on, or we'll be late!
Is the lorry filled with diesel? Will someone check the gate?
Have I forgotten something? Just check the list once more –
'Cause I just have this feeling – **Oh, Mum don't be a bore.**
One wrong turn, then another. This place is hard to find,
And this uneasy feeling is still growing in my mind.
Hooray, at last we've made it. Just in time to walk the course.
And I KNOW what I've forgotten – YES –
   the flippin' HORSE!

Shirley Cruickshank

TESTING TIME

Walking down the centre line, I think so far so good,
I wonder if that buck will count, I don't see why it should.
I think we cut that corner, he didn't want to go in there,
Well, he really is the wrong shape if I try to ride a square.

What comes next, the horn blows, the judge says we went wrong—
never knew three minutes could've lasted quite as long!
Serpentine from off the track, I think we're way too wide—
And someone said five metre loops don't touch the other side!

Working canter — I can't stop — will someone help me please?
What a leap, did you see that, we cleared that car with ease.
No, don't jump the white bits that are lying on the floor,
And free walk doesn't always mean you can drag me to the door.

Nearly there, remember at the X we have to stop—
I think we got a bit too close, I saw her score sheets drop!
That sliding halt that we put in should gain a mark or two—
And show them that we're versatile, and that we do Western too!

I wonder if we've won it, when the sheets come in we'll see,
But even if we aren't first we'll be in the top three.
What's this? Rows of zeros, that judge she wasn't well:
Her face was white as we went past, and that's how I can tell.

I read the judge's comment, not to worry, try again,
That's cool because I've entered the next test— Prelim 10.
The judge she gets her entry list, she glances up at me,
She flings the car door open, and across the school does flee.

Extra time to warm us up, that sure will come in handy,
I hear two words, one is my name, the other one sounds like
brandy.
The judge returns, her writer too, more confident by far,
They've now got neat square bales of hay stacked all around their car.
That judge is a comedienne I'm really sure of that,
She's back with body armour on, and wearing a hard hat!

Shirley Cruickshank

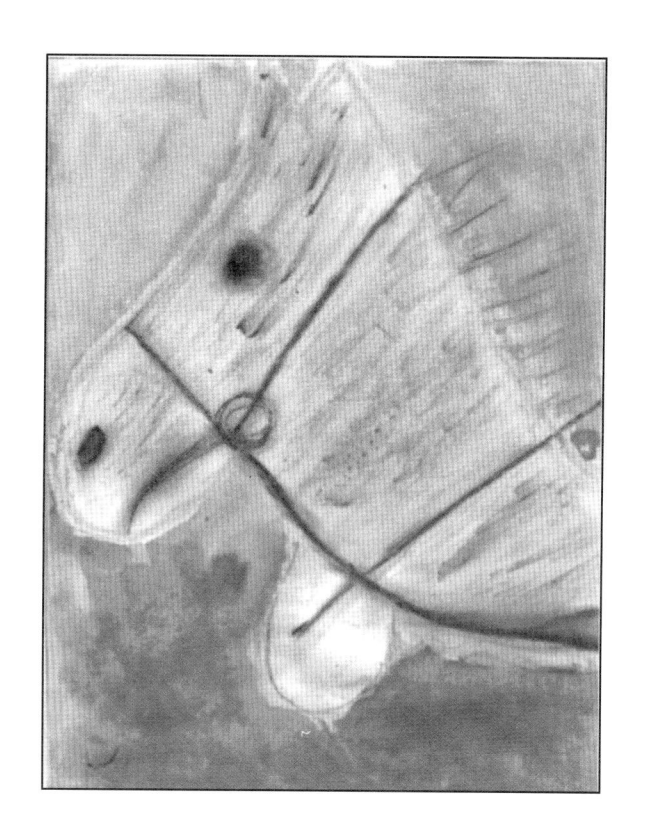

Grant Cooper (Age 9)
RDA Rider

THE GRAND FUND RAISING AUCTION

The day has come and tempers fray,
We all proceed with caution.
What is it that looms over us?
The Grand Fund Raising Auction.

Pots and pans and ironing boards,
Sofas chairs and mugs,
Wellie boots and woolly socks
And two moth-eaten rugs.

Fishing rods and Grandpa's teeth,
The contents of our homes,
Old picture frames, a worn string vest
And countless garden gnomes.

A riding hat, some old horse shoes,
A bag of chicken mash,
Four mousetraps and an old bee hive,
All there to raise some cash.

An old stone 'Pig', a box of nails,
A real four-poster bed,
Three flying ducks, china dog,
A plastic horse's head.

The end has come, a pile of cash,
But, oh what is that racket?
The busy Auctioneer has sold
Our Chairman's Gucci jacket.

Jean Emslie
RDA Driver

WISH YOU WERE HERE

Holidays are here again, two weeks of sand and sun,
But already I don't want to go, my horse is much more fun.
We sit aboard the aircraft, the stewardess hurries round,
How dare she bother me with lunch when I'm reading
    Horse and Hound!
We step down onto burning soil, the sun so bright outside,
Thank goodness I don't live here, it's far too hot to ride.
Lazing there down on the beach, to most the view is fine,
but to me those rocks are markers and that stone's the
    Centre line.
I watch as lovers stroll along, doing things that lovers do,
While the only thing that's on my mind is learning Prelim 2!
First one Thursday then the next, I'm all sunburned and red,
I keep thinking how I'd rather be at Riding Club instead.
Soon we start the packing, for it's nearly time to go,
I should be washing Jene at home, getting ready for the show.
The last day finally comes around — I knew it would, of course,
Once again I settle in the plane with a copy of 'Your Horse'.
We're nearly home— soon see your horse, says hubby, being
kind.
What horse? I say, **Oh, MY horse! Gosh, she's never crossed
my mind!**

THE HORSE OWNER'S YEAR!

Like soldiers, the wellies line up in my hall,
While pieces of harness adorn the wall.
There's footprints and hay seeds all over the floor,
Wax jackets and oilskins are hung on the door.
It won't be this bad once the winter is past—
Surely this cold and wet weather won't last.
At last muddy winter it gives way to spring,
With all of the problems we know it will bring.
The hours that we spend grooming out that dead hair,
Riding horses, so fresh, now that spring's in the air.
The daylight hours lengthen, the grass starts to grow,
How I'll fasten that girth, I really don't know.
With summer the smell's of the newly mown hay,
Hot sun, when the horses stand in for the day.
Pleased to be out in the cool of the night,
Grazing in peace, without midges that bite.
The usual panic of going to the shows—
Is it worth it I wonder— oh goodness knows.
To come home so tired, something's always 'unfair',
They shouldn't have won that, the judge bred that mare!
Suddenly evenings are getting quite grey,
A chilly night air, autumn's fast on its way.
The evenings grow darker, it's not safe to ride,
And riding club meetings again move inside.
Rain and cold sleet are now starting to fall,
And rows of green wellies are now back in my hall!!!

Shirley Cruickshank

BUT!

The thing about it is,
I can't make up my mind...
I don't know what to say or do;
The only word that fits is BUT...
What do you think?

Lindsey Telfar
Contributor

MY BLACK EYE

It was sore.

It is sore.

I swore.

People stare.

I don't care.

I hit the stair.

Sick.

Now.

I will take care.

Linda Lawrie
Contributor

PHANTOM GIPSY

The night is still, the insects are humming.
A sound from the distance, a quiet guitar strumming.
Flickering light, from a campfire that's burning.
I peer through the bushes, my heart full of yearning.
Caravans sit in a circle of splendour,
A young man sings songs to his loved one so tender.
Animals too, there are horses and dogs,
Children are playing and men chopping logs.
The babies are quiet now, they all are asleep,
Closer and closer I feel I must creep.
The songs become clearer, the music more loud,
Around the bright campfire has gathered a crowd.
Then she appeared in ribbons and gold,
Dancing and whirling, a story she told
Of life as a Gipsy travelling the land;
The tambourine glistened like jewels in her hand.
Her man sat beside her, playing his tune,
He played and she danced in the light of the moon.
When they were ended, their songs had been sung—
In my mind I still heard how the tambourine rung.
I must have been weary, for I clapped my hand,
And I seem to have frightened my travelling band.
They stared and they shivered, they turned ghostly white,
They all seemed to vanish just into the night.
So slowly I ventured out into the place,
No Gipsies, nor caravans, now just empty space.
Surely I dreamt all the sights I had seen,
But wait— there's hot ash where the campfire has been!

Shirley Cruickshank

THE AFTERMATH

He stands alone, his shoulders hunched, his eyes are brimmed with tears
As he thinks of all the struggles he has weathered through the years.
He stares out through the window, hears a shot, then two, then three—
And knows that his worst nightmare has become reality.
Disinfectant mingles now with death's sweet sickly smell,
Just how long will this go on, if only he could tell.
For miles around the evening sky is lit by glowing flames,
He knows that life for him at least will never be the same.
Carcasses of the stock he loved, the mound is growing higher,
He must wait for machines to come and place them on the pyre.
Stress takes its toll on farming folks, some will leave their wives,
Many will be destitute and some will take their lives.
He knows they have to do it, but still he wonders why,
If there's a God that cares, why did they all have to die?
No calves are suckling from the cows, no ewes lamb in the shed,
On the green fields' grizzly mountains, all of them lie dead.
The months have passed, a summer shower falls gently on the ground,
The distant clop of horses hooves is now the only sound.
His life is empty, like his farm, tears like a river run,
As he drives off in his tractor, beside him is his gun.

Shirley Cruickshank

CLIP CLOP

Clip clop
Trip trop
My horse hooves are moving
Feel the horse's coat
My horse is smooth and warm
Clip clop
Trip trop
My horse's nostrils snuffling
Leaves rustling
Footsteps walk in time
Clip clop
Trip trop
Dancing lights are flashing
Through the tree tops
Feeling proud on lovely Buzby.

Rhys Leslie
RDA Rider

Wait for Me'

Michael Smith (Age 13)
RDA Rider

COPPER'S CHRISTMAS LIGHTS

Twelve Christmas lights on the tree
One for each year you spent with me
You must have been sent from above
For you gave such undying love
No greater gift could anyone receive?
My heart knows how to grieve

So hard it was to let you go
No more hoof-prints in the falling snow
As Christmas lights shine bright
My thoughts are with you every night
For all the time spent together
My love for you will be forever.

Doris Moore
RDA Helper

LAST CHRISTMAS

It's Christmas morning, Kate she rises,
parcels full of lovely surprises.
The little girl is pony mad
and doted on by mum and dad.

Her presents now she opens up,
jodhpurs, hat and horsey cup.
A tabard saying 'horse and rider',
the tension builds up now inside her...

She hears a noise outside the door,
the tabard gets tossed to the floor.
A chestnut mare is standing there,
sun glinting on its golden hair.

Please can I ride her now? asks Kate,
Of course, but darling don't be late.
She clambers up and rides away
thinking what her friends will say...

She called on everyone she could
and stayed out longer than she should.
The sun had gone, the sky turned grey,
when she said goodbye and rode away.

The snowstorm came before they got far
and the blizzard hid them from the car.
Now child and pony both lie dead—
ghostly white against chestnut red.

While underneath the Christmas tree
the tabard glows for all to see.

Shirley Cruickshank

WORKING IN A WINTER WONDER YARD

(to the tune Winter Wonderland)

<u>Chorus</u>
In the yard, snow is glistening,
I need a hand, but no-one's listening.
I've no time to yap, even though the pay's crap ___
I'm working in a winter wonder yard.

1.

All the beds must be done to perfection,
Every blade of straw swept up outside.
Feed and tack rooms all must be made tidy,
For the owners who turn up just to ride.

<u>Chorus</u>

2.

They only stay an hour and they cause havoc,
Complain about the way I get things done.
I'd like to slap them hard but I keep smiling,
'Cause after all, horse-owning should be fun!

<u>Chorus</u>

3.

Then they ask if I could do a favour?
Could I pull some manes and trim some tails?
I check my hat to see if MUG is written—
I suppose there is the dole if all else fails.

Chorus

4.

Christmas Day I try to finish early,
Yes, I cut some corners here and there.
But if the owners tell the Boss about it,
Remember that in war all things are fair!

Chorus
Repeat chorus

Shirley Cruickshank

Jamie Penny (Age 13)
RDA Rider

CHRISTMAS WISH

"What do you want for Christmas, lad?" was what the Santa said.
I only want a pony— no, nothing else instead.
Not a new bike, nor an action man; a skateboard will not do,
I wrote it in my letter and I posted it to you.
"A pony is quite large, you know, to fit into my sack,
And what if there's a blizzard and the snow falls on his back?"
It doesn't matter if it snows, I've a place for him to stay,
There's straw for him to sleep on and a bale of clean sweet hay.
"Oh well", said Santa smiling, "You've clearly thought this through.
Now I can't promise anything but I'll see what I can do."
Christmas morning, out he ran just fast as he was able,
But all was as he'd left it in the neat and tidy stable.
As he walked back to the cottage, his face was wet with tears.
Then he heard a truck approaching, he could scarce believe his ears.
The rattle of a trailer as it bounced along behind.
He wondered what was in it, but he didn't really mind.
A Highland pony stood inside, a lovely yellow dun,
With a note tied on by Santa, saying, 'I hope this is the one.
I'm sorry that he wasn't there first thing on Christmas day,
But the best reindeer has taken ill, so he had to pull my sleigh!
Look after him, enjoy him, and he'll take care of you,
I wish you both the best of luck in every thing you do.'
Hugging his new pony, the little boy just knew
What he was going to name him— you've guessed it—
   Rudolph Two!

Shirley Cruickshank

OH WINTER TIME

(To the tune of Jingle Bells)

Chorus

Oh, Winter time, Winter time,
Out in snow and rain,
I wonder why I'm doing this,
I think I am insane.
Oh, Winter time, Winter time,
Chapped lips, drippy nose,
The only things I ever wear
Are boots and muddy clothes.

1.

Wading through the mud, the sleet is blowing hard,
Feed pails in my hands, I struggle through the yard.
Horses scrape and paw, while I struggle with the door,
My hands are so blooming cold, I drop food on the floor.

Chorus

2.

I try to rug them up, but they're anxious to get out,
One stands on my toes, just hear me scream and shout.
That's the last one out, they gallop off with glee,
I limp back, into the house, it's cuppa time for me.

Chorus

3.

Housework it needs done, but only what I must,
I cook and do the washing, but I don't disturb the dust.
Now back to muck them out, water, hay and feed,
No time to think of lunch for me, they must have what they need.

Chorus

4.

Finished now at last, I glance towards the gate,
They're all lined up to come back in, oh horses can't you wait?
It's almost four o'clock, the day is dark outside,
I've never stopped, I'm knackered and I've had no time to ride.

Chorus

Shirley Cruickshank

WINTER'S TALE

Spare me a thought this winter,
If you see me standing there,
Ice forming on my whiskers,
As the wind whips through my hair.
While you're snug and warm inside your house,
Watching your TV—
I'm out here in the freezing cold,
No luxuries for me.
Every time I hear a car,
Oh how my hopes run high!
Another one, and still not her,
I turn, and heave a sigh.
At last I hear it, that's the one—
My mum she's come for me!
I neigh, and canter to the gate—
This means it's time for tea!
Soon I'm tucked up in my bed
And stand there munching hay.
While darkness falls now all around,
Here ends another day.
I don't know who it was that said
That all cobs should be tough—
They lied.
A little while outside
in winter's long enough!!!

'JENE' Cruickshank

BOB THE COB

Have you met Bob the grumpy cob?
His feet are big and hairy,
His tail is long, his legs are strong,
And his one white eye is scary.
He does this trick, where he steals your stick
To make you think you've lost it.
And then next day, beneath the hay,
You'll find it where he's tossed it!
He likes to jump, but gets the hump
If you try to take him hacking—
He flattens his ears, and bucks and rears
And sends the others packing.
He loves his hay, and he'd eat all day—
And it doesn't seem to matter
If you go for a ride, or he stays inside,
He just keeps getting fatter!

Shirley Cruickshank

TWO POUNDS AND AN APPLE

Two pounds in my pocket
And an apple for Buzby
Going on the bus
Everyone is happy
Trotting through the trees
Feeling good.

Darryl Stephen (Age 9)
RDA Rider

Stacey Cheyne (Age 9)
RDA RIDER

JOIN THE GROUP

I offer here information
That may be of use to you
If you decide to join our Group
as Ben Hurs or Helpers too

The AB Whips teach us to drive
In spite of this they still survive
Their voices reach a higher pitch
As just in time we miss a ditch

We listen to these AB Whips
Our eyes alight with awe
They ought to hear the things we say
When they've gone through the door

The Helpers come in many guises
Large and small and medium sizes
They comfort us with TLC
Coffee biscuits chat and tea

They help us dress and keep us right
And say **Ponies rarely bite**
Besides the gig they keep their paces
With 'Huffs and Puffs' and reddened faces

That's really all that I can tell
I've made it kind and gentle
But if you want to join our Group
A sense of humour is essential.

Jean Emslie
RDA Driver

Richard Gray (Age 16)
RDA Rider

ABOUT SHIRLEY CRUICKSHANK

While I have always enjoyed writing poems for 'fun', it wasn't until I submitted a couple to my Riding Club Newsletter that I realised how popular they were, and how many other members appreciated them.

Over the years, many people have used my poems, for many purposes, and in many countries.

Most of the poems were written with specific horses in mind, but most people can relate to them— identifying perhaps with a particular horse, or an incident in their own lives. Maybe that's why so many of them tug at the heartstrings!

I live in the Northeast of Scotland with my partner, two dogs and two horses. My two grown-up children (a son and daughter) also live in this area. Aberdeenshire Council employs me as a full time Car Park Operative, but in addition to the domestic chores and caring for the animals, I still manage to make time for my other great love, which is belly dancing. I have studied this dance form for several years now, and it's a great way to keep fit!

I was only too glad to be able to help the RDA fundraise with the publication of this book, and I hope everyone finds a special something within these pages, a poem that will become 'your poem'. Thank you for buying this book. Please enjoy it, and know that you have helped support one of the greatest charities around.